A BOOT UP

DARTMOOR'S SITES
OF MAGIC & MYSTERY

John Earle

First published in Great Britain in 2011

British Library Cataloguing-in-Publication Data
A CIP record for this title is available from the British Library

ISBN 978 0 85710 038 2

PiXZ Books
Halsgrove House, Ryelands Industrial Estate,
Bagley Road, Wellington, Somerset TA21 9PZ
Tel: 01823 653777
Fax: 01823 216796
email: sales@halsgrove.com

An imprint of Halstar Ltd, part of the Halsgrove group of companies
Information on all Halsgrove titles is available at: www.halsgrove.com

Printed and bound in China by Toppan Leefung Printing Ltd

Contents

Dartmoor's Sites of Magic & Mystery

How to use this book

The Area

When you have been out walking on Dartmoor have you ever had that feeling that you were not alone and that eyes were secretly watching you? Or perhaps you have had a strange, cold feeling that made you shiver and shudder even on a warm day, as if some restless spirit was passing by?

It is no wonder that mysterious Dartmoor with its sudden mists and sucking, quaking bogs, prehistoric tombs, deserted farms and abandoned mines has a great many legends and folk tales of ghosts, witches, even pixies! Many of them, of course, are to explain some of the weird features of the moor, or to give an explanation to some unaccountable, sinister occurrence but I still feel a strange prickling sensation in my scalp when I am alone in one of the mystifying stone circles or rows or wandering in one of the moss-covered, ancient, ruined farms. I can almost sense the spirits of the ancient people of Dartmoor with their stories and histories. While near the deserted ghostly mines I think that perhaps that I can hear the clang of the hammers and shovels and a low murmur of the miners' voices going about their work.

Then there are the remains of the medieval villages whose inhabitants were decimated by the Black Death; I always feel a sad and ghostly presence there, full of deep sorrow.

The Walks

The walks in this book are themselves interesting but they will all take you to areas of the moor that are associated with a number of the weird and mysterious legends and stories, from prehistory to modern times, of this haunting, beautiful landscape.

A word of warning: Dartmoor is a high, dangerous upland area where the weather can change in moments and, of course, you will have heard of the sudden mists and the quaking bogs. What I am saying is that you must wear the right clothes and boots. You need to take warm sweaters or fleeces, a hat and gloves and really good waterproofs, even in summer. A small rucksack is useful to carry spare clothing if its a warm day, food for the day, a water bottle or Thermos, a torch and whistle, and a small first aid kit might also come in handy.

The Maps

While there are sketch maps in this book you really do need to be able to read and use a map and compass. The best one, but it is quite large and awkward to use on wet and windy days, is the Outdoor Leisure 28 Series also known as the Explorer Series for Dartmoor. The scale is 1:25 000, 4cm to 1km or 2.5 inches to the mile. Or there is the Landranger Series with a scale of 1:50 000, 2cm to 1km or 1.25 inches to 1 mile. You will need Sheets 191 and 202 to cover both north and south Dartmoor.

All the walks except one are circular but it is quite possible to shorten some of them by cutting off corners or starting at a different place to the one I suggest. I am not giving the time each walk takes as everyone walks at a different pace and, also, I hope that you will not want to rush around as fast as you can so that you ponder about the ghosts and feel the presence of the spirits of the old people.

Also I hope that you will have time to drop into some of the pubs, inns and café that are mentioned in this book.

And a final warning. Watch out for the pixies. They lived in tiny, turf-covered huts and knew the secret ways through bogs, marshes and peat hags. They could melt away into the wild moor carrying with them stolen cattle, children and womenfolk – watch out for your wives and daughters! They were responsible for all kinds of tricks and practical jokes such as leading men astray when coming home late from the market, stealing horses to have races and making people dance all night in their fairy rings. Good walking!

Useful telephone numbers

Dartmoor National Park Authority. 01626 832093 • The Dartmoor Trust which runs the Dartmoor Archive (pictures of Dartmoor on line) see www.dartmoorarchive.org. Office 01752 837265 • High Moorland Visitor Centre. Princetown 01822 890414 • Weather Forecasts 0891 500404 • Firing on Dartmoor Ranges. Freephone. 0800 458 4868

Key to Symbols Used

Level of difficulty:

Easy 🖤

Fair 🖤 🖤

More challenging 🖤 🖤 🖤

Map symbols:

🚗 Park & start

    Road

- - - Walk Footpath

■ Building / Town

+ Church

▲ Landmark

🚻 WC

🍴 Refreshments

🍺 Pub

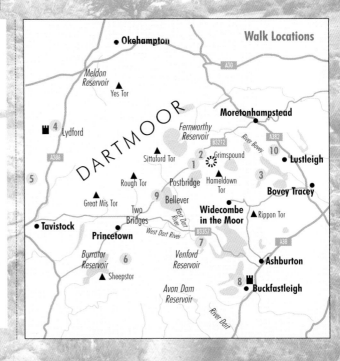

Walk Locations

● Okehampton

Meldon Reservoir

▲ Yes Tor

A30

Moretonhampstead ●

♜ 4 Lydford

Fernworthy Reservoir

B3212

River Bovey   A382

D A R T M O O R

2 Grimspound

10

● **Lustleigh**

A386

▲ Sittaford Tor

1

Hamledown Tor

5

▲ Rough Tor

Postbridge

3

Bovey Tracey ●

9 Bellever

▲ Great Mis Tor

Two Bridges

East Dart River

Widecombe in the Moor

▲ Rippon Tor

● **Tavistock**

Princetown

West Dart River   B3357

7

A38

Burrator Reservoir

6

Venford Reservoir

● **Ashburton**

▲ Sheepstor

8 ♜ **Buckfastleigh**

Avon Dam Reservoir

River Dart

6

1 The Body in the Chest

Start at a pub with a history, visit an old mine and a medieval village before climbing back to the pub.

Level: 🥾 🥾
Length: 4.5 miles.
Terrain: Mainly tracks across moorland and fields.
Park and Start: ref. SX676811
Refreshments: The Warren House Inn.

What better place to start and end a walk than at a car park just down the road from a pub and no ordinary pub at that. The Warren House Inn is supposed to be the third highest pub in Britain, and as the name suggests it was once a house where a warrener lived, before it became a pub, who made a living by breeding and trapping rabbits for both fur and meat in artificial burrows. In fact the building was on the other side of the road in the early days and you can see the ruins. When it opened as a pub it was used a lot by the miners from all the mines, the ruins of which you can see all around you.

It is a cosy pub and it is said that the open fire that burnt peat in the old days has not been out for a hundred years; they just rekindle the glowing ashes from the logs each day.

A Dartmoor story before you start your walk. It was a dark and stormy night and the snowdrifts around the Warren House Inn were so deep that a traveller realized that he would never get off the moor that night so he asked for a night's lodging at the

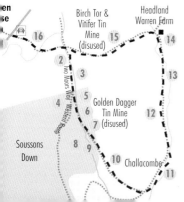

The Warren House Inn.

Inn. After a good meal and great hospitality he was shown to his bedroom. In the corner of the room there was a huge chest and unable to resist his curiosity he peeped inside. You can imagine his horror when he saw, laid out in it, the body of an old man. He spent the rest of the night lying awake shaking with fear, believing the innkeepers were murderers who killed their guests for their money. Pale and weary the next morning he staggered down to breakfast and plucked up enough courage to ask the landlady about the body in the chest. "Why bless you." she said. "Never you fear, tis only grandfer. He died a few weeks back and what with the weather being so bad and the ground frozen hard, we have not been able to bury him so we salted him down as we do with the bacon. When the weather improves we shall take him down to Widecombe to bury him."

1 If you can leave the fire and the beer, go back to the car park and set off down the track.

2 At the bottom of the hill you will see that the track bends to the left but you can cut the corner off by going steeply down on a rough eroded path to the grassy area with ruins all around.

Ruins at Vitifer Mine.

Redwater Brook at Vitifer Mine.

3 You are now standing near to what was once one of the busiest mining areas on Dartmoor; the Vitifer and Birch Tor Mines. Tin had been extracted here from early times but by 1738 there were over 13 shafts some over 40 fathoms deep; mine depths are always given in fathoms.

4 There are many ruined buildings but one of them is a Miners' Dry where the miners, after their shift underground, would

It is said that in the Great Blizzard of 1891 it was possible to step out of the bedroom windows of the miners' cottages on to the deep snow

try to get warm and change their clothes and dry the ones they had been wearing all day as these mines were notoriously wet. It was said that they cut holes in the toes of their boots so that the water could run out!

5 Cross the little granite bridge over Redwater Brook. The stream probably got its name because of the minerals in the water. Turn right and follow the track south down the valley.

6 Go though the gate into Soussons Forest. You are now in another mining area – the Golden Dagger Mine. The hill that rises to the west is Dagger Hill. A possible explanation of the origins of the names is that a Bronze Age dagger was found near here and perhaps the bronze was mistaken for gold.

7 Nothing but ghostly ruins remain of the main mine buildings, the stamping mills and the smith's shop. As there was up the valley at Vitifer, there is another Miners' Dry and there are stories told that if you come here at dusk you can hear a mysterious low murmur of voices and a strange musty smell of wet clothes that drifts in the still air.

8 Most of the shafts, adits and gullies have disappeared in the conifer plantations that now cover the area but if you look up right as you walk on down the left hand track you can see the Dagger or Stamps wheel pit and the leat that carried the water to power the giant wheels.

Dinah's House.

9 Keep walking south and you will pass Dinah's House on your right where some of the miners lived though it's not clear who Dinah was. People lived here until 1940.

Next on your left you will see the remains of an engine house that brought power to the mine. Finally on your right is a buddle. There are quite a few of these on Dartmoor where crushed tin ore in water was fed over the central core or boss. The heavier particles of tin

Remains of Golden Dagger Mine.

Foundations for machinery in the old engine house.

settled in the centre near the core while the lighter debris floated to the outer rim. There were several long arms with brushes attached that rotated to prevent channels forming and to mix the ore. These strange machines were the modern mechanical way of panning and streaming for ores with a large bowl as they did in the old days.

What an amazing mining area this is, and incredibly mining went on here until between the two wars and only stopped production in the 1920s.

(10) Walk to the gate on the left and follow the path along the south edge of Challacombe Down. See the bluebells in May

(11) The path then swings north and goes through a gate and a deep track down to Challacombe Farm and the remains of a medieval village. Keep an eye out for the tinners' mould stone. Certainly Bronze Age people lived around here but in medieval times there was a thriving little village of about 12 houses. You will see the ruins ahead of you after the farm.

(12) Go north through the gate past Challacombe Cottages and then another gate that will lead you onto grassy meadows. To your right by a sycamore tree there are the ruins of a water mill by the small stream of the West Webbern. As you walk up the broad valley look left and you can make out the remains of the medieval strip lynchets. These are terraces that were made by ploughing with oxen along the side of the hill.

Medieval Village Challacombe.

Tinners' mould stone at Challacombe.

The mine gullies or gerts above Headland Warren.

13 A gentle climb now and if you look down right you might make out the remains of a wheel pit which powered the pumping rods of East Birch Tor Mine. Keep an eye out too for the remains of a leat and the gullies that held the pumping rods that worked the pumps for water in the shafts of the nearby mines.

14 On past Headland Warren Farm on the right of way (see Walk 2 for details about this remote farm).

15 Turn left and start the climb up west on the eroded path.

On the other side of the col you pass near a series of deep gullies (again see the Walk 2 for details of these.)

16 You will soon reach the bottom of the valley and Vitifer Mine again so follow the track that you came down back to the car park and maybe make another visit to the Warren House Inn.

2 **A Night Trapped Down a Mine Shaft**

A pack of cards, evil creatures below ground, a miner's pub and a near disaster.

N ear the Car Park you will see Bennett's Cross marking an old track across the moor from Moretonhampstead as well as the boundaries of Chagford and North Bovey. It has WB cut into it to mark the bondmark for Warren Bounds or possibly for William Bennett (Bennet) who was a juror in the Tinners' Parliament on Crockern Tor in the reign of Henry VIII (see Walk 9) and was connected to the stannary of Chagford.

Across the valley you will see two stone enclosures. One is shaped like a heart and the other like a diamond on a pack of cards. These are said to

Level: 🥾 🥾
Length: 2.5 miles or 4 miles.
Terrain: Tracks across moorland.
Park and Start: Ref. SX681817
Refreshments: The Warren House Inn.

be the playing cards of the wicked tinner Jan Reynolds that were dropped by him when he was carried off by the Devil for playing cards during the sermon in Widecombe Church one Sunday. There was a flash of lighting that broke one of the spires followed by a thunder clap and ferocious winds and Jan was never seen again.

Two Moors Way
Undefined

① ⑦ ⑥

Bennett's Cross

Two Moors Way Central Route

Two Moors Way
Western Route

▲ Birch Tor

⑤ Hameldown Tor ▲

Birch Tor & Vitifer Tin Mine (disused)

④ ■

② Headland Warren Farm ③

en Inn

13

The diamond of Jan Reynolds' pack of cards.

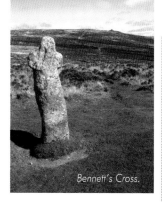

Bennett's Cross.

The ruins of the miners' barracks.

Enough of Dartmoor stories, so set off more or less south keeping well to the right to avoid the huge gullies or gerts and down steeply to the valley floor. Keep an eye out for the deep, flooded very overgrown wheel pit on your right. A leat ran for seven miles to bring water to this and other wheels. You now pass a number of ruins to your left which were the barracks where the miners lived, a smelting house, a smithy and dressing floors of Vitifer and Birch Tor Mines. You have now linked up with Walk 1 so you can find further details of the mining there.

Start to climb up to the left on the track that leaves the valley floor. You will soon be in an area of huge gullies or gerts. One particularly deep ravine is known as Chaw Gulley. Chaw is possibly the corruption of Chough, the rare Cornish bird associated with King Arthur that

Mine gullies or gerts.

once flew here. In the past there was a deep mine here that was said to produce rich seams of gold as well as tin. Fortune seekers would enter the shafts on ropes looking for the gold nuggets that were supposed to be hidden in the damp, dank depths. There are stories told that there were evil, subterranean creatures who guarded the gold. Suddenly a slimy hand would dart out in the darkness and push the unsuspecting explorers to their deaths down the deep shaft. The next morning the corpses would be laid out by the entrance to the mine as a warning. There are many stories about deformed, malevolent creatures haunting mines all over the world and on Dartmoor they are called "Knockers". On quiet moonless nights if you go near the shafts and adits of

Bennett's Cross is one of over 130 granite crosses to be found on Dartmoor. Many are said to have been erected as waymarkers by monks to guide travellers across the moor.

the old mines you can hear them deep down tapping with their hammers and if you are unlucky they will emerge to kidnap you like the pixies.

 At the top of the hill, if you felt like it, you could follow a

Triple Stone Row.

Headland Warren.

track off to the right to have a look at an outstanding triple stone row.

(4) On down the track now towards Headland Warren Farm. The building dates back to the thirteenth century and was a pub for the thirsty miners of Headland Mine and the Birch Tor and Vitifer Mines. It was known as Birch Tor Inn. A sign used to hang outside that said "Jan Roberts lives here. Sells cider and beer. Your hearts for to cheer; And if you want meat. To make up a treat. Here be rabbits to eat."

Another owner of Headland Warren was James Hannaford who, returning from the Warren House Inn one dark night, fell down one of the many mine shafts in the area. Somehow his fall was stopped by a wooden platform some way below the surface but it was too far down and too difficult to be able to climb out. His faithful collie waited all night whimpering and whining by the deep hole. Daylight came and the search parties set out to look for James as word had got around that he was missing. After a considerable time, attracted and guided by the collie's barks they were able to haul the old man out. James Hannaford never forgot that he owed his life to his faithful dog. James was

quite badly crippled by his night in the shaft and there are stories told now of a mysterious man seen, with a collie by his side, limping across the misty moor at dusk.

(5) Follow the track that climbs up north east towards the road. If you have not visited it before you might like to climb straight on to the road and just before Firth Bridge

follow the track up left to Grimspound. This is one of the finest Bronze Age settlements on Dartmoor with a great enclosing wall and hut circles.

(6) If you don't want to go to Grimspound then walk up left on the broad track and just before the road take a sharp left turn across the moor. This path will lead you to the Two Moors Way that splendid journey

Ruined shelter on the Two Moors Way.

you can make from Dartmoor to Exmoor. Turn left onto it. The other interesting local long distance path is the Mariners' Way that goes from Dartmouth to Bideford which sailors used when changing ships. This route runs slightly further east from here.

(7) Climb over the crest of the hill near Birch Tor past the little stone shelter and down the other side back to Bennett's Cross

The path back.

3 Wish Hounds and the Hunter

*Mysterious hounds, a village decimated by
the Black Death, a stone man and a suicide*

There is a large car park at the foot of Hound Tor and refreshments are usually available - in summer months at least - at the hot dog stall aptly and amusingly called "Hound of the Basketmeals".

The tor itself is one of the most dramatic on Dartmoor and, as a result, it is associated with many fascinating stories and legends.

In recent times vandals pushed over one of the rock pinnacles but this has done little to alter the outline of the tor which has all the look of a giant's ruined castle towering over the surrounding moorland.

Level: 🐾 🐾
Length: 4 miles
Terrain: Open moor and lanes.
Park and Start: Ref. SX739792
Refreshments: Refreshment stall in summer.

The refreshment stall at Hound Tor car park.

1. Set off up the gentle slope towards the towering rocks of Hound Tor looking like a magic castle on top of the hill. This has always been my favourite tor with its grassy avenues running through sheer granite walls. Great blocks of rock, pillars and cracks where it is great for just exploring and clambering about while there are some exciting hard rock climbs. There is cave just round to the left on the north side that you squeeze into and emerge higher up. See if you can see the rocks that look like a hound that gave the tor its name. Some stories suggest that the whole tor looks like The Bowerman's pack of hounds turned to stone by witches; see later.

Dartmoor is full of legends of baying coal-black hounds, the Wish Hounds

Hound Tor.

and their phantom huntsmen, often the Devil, and other spectral, eerie black dogs hunting down their victims to death. On a sinister misty day it is easy to imagine, up here, in the alleys between the rocks, that you are being tracked across the desolate moor by a huge, malignant, black hound!

2 Walk on down the hill on the obvious path towards Greator Rocks.

Fireplace in the ruins of the medieval village.

Soon you will reach a number of low walls and foundations. These are the remains of the medieval village of the Manor of Hundatora. People lived here from the 10th to the 14th century and you can make out the foundations of the houses with fire-places and ovens for drying corn and barns for storage. All around there are the remains of the banks and walls of ancient field systems. There is even a corn ditch to keep out deer and other animals. The whole village was

Bluebells near Greator Rocks.

Medieval village at Hound Tor.

thought to have been abandoned at the time of the Black Death in 1348. People talk about hearing heart-rending weeping if you come here at dusk. It is a sad but fascinating place.

(3) Set off north from the deserted village down to the road by the corner of the wall.

(4) Turn right along the road. This is a delightful lane that runs down between walls and woods. The lane follows some right angle bends past the lovely old thatched farm of Great Houndtor with a barn bunkhouse. Keep on past Southcott until you reach Hayne Cross.

(5) Turn left up the lane to Hayne and follow the right of way through the fields to emerge on the open moor of Hayne Down.

The barn bunkhouse at Great Houndtor.

Great Houndtor Farmhouse.

6 Aim south-west across the moor. Off to your right you can see a fantastic isolated granite tower called the Bowerman's Nose. It has been suggested that the name comes from the Celtic words "vawr maen" which means large stone.

However a man called Bowerman lived near Hound Tor in the time of the Conqueror who was a fine archer or "bowman" and also a great hunter. One day with his hounds in full cry he galloped into a coven of witches making fearful spells. They

From Hayne Down you can look down over the village of Manaton. In the churchyard here is a granite cross around which the villagers once thrice carried their dead before burial. A Victorian vicar, outraged by this pagan practice, hid the cross, only for it to be discovered and re-erected in more recent (and enlightened) times!

were so furious that the next time Bowerman went out hunting one of the witches turned herself into a hare and led him on and on until he eventually collapsed into a bog. With a great shriek the witch turned him into stone as you can see. As for his hounds, well you have already seen them turned to stone at Hound Tor!

Bowerman's Nose.

The Wish Hounds and the Hunter

3

(7) Eventually you will reach the road and the moor gate. Walk left through the iron gate across the road and then immediately right through the small wooden gateway to reach the right of way across some fields and the edge of the moor to another road. On the opposite side you will see a grave. This is Jay's Grave. Kitty Jay was a poor country girl who was seduced by the son of the farm where she worked over 200 years ago. Full of shame and despair at being pregnant she hanged herself in a barn at Canna Farm near Easdon Farm. As was the custom of those days she was not allowed to be buried on consecrated ground so she was buried here at this crossing of old tracks. In 1860 a Mr James Bryant excavated the grave and found the bones of poor Kitty Jay and put them in a coffin and the reburied them raising the mound with the stones that you see today. It is said that there are always fresh flowers to be found on Jay's Grave and nobody knows who puts them there.

On moonlit summer nights sometimes a dark figure is seen kneeling mourning by the grave. Is it Kitty Jay or maybe the repentant son of the farmer keeping watch over the grave of his lover and their unborn child?

(8) Turn left and walk back beside the road to your car with Hound Tor looming above you.

Jay's Grave.

4 **The Ghost of Judge Jeffries**

An ancient castle and dungeon, Saxons, Vikings and a watchmaker's strange memorial

This is more of a wander than a walk. It is hard to imagine that Lydford was probably once one of the most important small towns in Devon. In a well defended position the Celtic people were the first to settle here

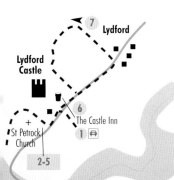

and even pottery from the Mediterranean has been discovered on archaeological digs. Britons defended it against the Cornish. There is even a strange rumour that Julius Caesar visited Lydford. It was a fortified town or burh in the Saxon Kingdom of Wessex ruled over by King Alfred. The Vikings, as mentioned in the Anglo-Saxon Chronicles, invaded the town. The Normans built a castle nearby and in 1195 Richard I ordered a stone keep to be built and this was called Lydford Castle the remains of which are now

Level: 🥾
Length: Less than a mile.
Terrain: Paths.
Park and Start: Ref. SX510847.
Refreshments: The Castle Inn or the Dartmoor Inn.

buried in the mound below the castle that you can see today.

On top of the original walls hidden in the mound, that became the foundations, the present castle was built in the thirteenth century. From earliest times the keep became a prison both for the king's prisoners and also those breaking the strict laws of the stannary and forests courts that were held here. It had a terrible and notorious reputation for handing out rigorous and cruel punishment usually hanging people without a fair trial.

By the time we get to James II there are stories told of the notorious Judge Jeffries sitting in judgement here. There is a belief on Dartmoor that those who have led wicked and evil lives should come back to haunt the areas where they lived, as black dogs, to expiate their awful crimes. Judge Jeffries was so terrible that he is said to be seen by the villagers not as a black dog but as a black pig haunting the scenes of his Bloody Assizes of Lydford.

You can wander round the castle and peep inside and walk in the courtyard behind. It is all in an excellent state of preservation and it is easy to imagine the wretched prisoners awaiting their fate, probably hanging, locked in this ancient and notorious castle.

The daunting Lydford Castle.

2 Go back to the road and look out for a gate on your right that goes between the castle and the church. Keep an eye out for the Viking stone to commemorate their invasion of AD 997. Walk round the church-yard until you come to the end of the

The ditch and ramparts of the Norman Castle.

The stone commemorating the Viking invasion of Lydford in AD 997.

promontory on which Lydford was built with a steep drop down to the gorge below. The Saxon ramparts were built here that kept the Vikings out. On the steepest part of the slope down to the gorge the Normans also built a wooden castle in the

eleventh century on top of a motte with a surrounding ditch and ramparts. There would have been a wall enclosing the main area of the keep and remains of five little houses have been found inside by archaeologists.

(3) Walk back to the road and then enter the churchyard to visit the church. It may seem odd to have a church in Devon named after the Cornish saint St Petrock or Petroc. But this saint, who was said to have been a Welsh prince, gave up his royal upbringing to study religion in Ireland with the many other Celtic saints, and in a vision was told to go to Cornwall. After a stormy crossing of the Irish Sea he landed at the Camel Estuary in the sixth century and built

'Lydford Law' became a bye-word for injustice - as the local rhyme has it:
"I oft have heard of Lydford Law, How in the morn they hang and draw, And sit in judgement after."

St Petrock's Church.

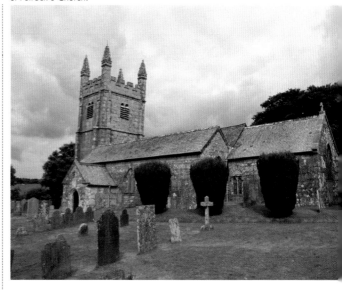

his first church at Lanwethinoc that became Padstow. He travelled extensively in the west of England founding many churches including this one at Lydford and it is said that he even got as far as Rome and Jerusalem.

St Anne: stained glass in the church.

15th century Flemish glass.

Many legends about him survive; of how he turned water into nectar and tamed a terrible dragon that was plundering the Cornish coast.

A church was here in the 6th century and by 1237 just after Lydford Castle was built there is reference to a stone church which was enlarged in 1262, and later again leading up to 1428 it was further enlarged and the tower built.

(4) There is much to see inside the church including some Flemish glass from the fifteenth century, a pre-Norman font made of Hurdwick stone, pews with carved

ends donated by the late Duke of Windsor when he was Duke of Cornwall.

(5) On your way out look for the watchmaker's tomb near the porch on your left. George Routledge was a watchmaker who died in 1802 and the long epitaph carved on the tomb amusingly plays with words to do with clocks and watches to describe his life.

The pleasant Castle Inn.

The Watchmaker's Tomb.

(6) Walk on now past the Castle Inn and follow the main street until you can see the Town Bank on either side which would have blocked the entrance to the promontory and which were put up by Alfred in Angle Saxon times. Built two centuries before the Normans arrived this was part of the ramparts surrounding the whole of Alfred's original burgh.

(7) You can return to the car park (or the inn) by following a path that runs round inside the ramparts to your left, on the north-west side of the main street.

5 The Work of the Devil at Brent Tor

*Legend of the Gubbings, the building of
St Michael's church in spite of the devil*

As with the previous excursion at Lydford this is only a short walk with a steep climb, but before you set off you might like to hear about the legend of Gubbings-land.

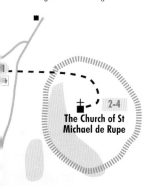

**The Church of St
Michael de Rupe**

2-4

The derogatory word gubbings means shavings of fish and was used by a Thomas Fuller in about 1650 to describe a group of outlaws who lived near Brent Tor. He wrote "that some two hundred years since, two strumpets being with child, fled thither to hide themselves, to whom certain lewd fellow resorted." It appears that in the sixteenth century a hoard of red-bearded Gubbinses terrified the area around Brent Tor. They survived by killing and robbing and rustling sheep

Level:
Length: Under a mile
Terrain: Track and path.
Park & start: Ref. SX469805
Refreshments: Mary Tavy & Peter Tavy
or Tavistock.

and cattle then disappearing into the labyrinth of little glens and gullies around here where they could not be traced. The leader was eventually killed near the Dartmoor Inn that you might have visited on the last walk.

1 The church of St Michael stands high above you as you cross the road from the car park to go through the gate and join the obvious track that climbs the hill. St Michael is traditionally the saint of high places, where he is said to have defeated evil. The embodiment of evil in paintings of this triumph is often depicted as a dragon lunging out at him from swirling clouds.

Brent Tor seen for miles around.

(2) As you walk up the track with the church looming above you it becomes obvious that this mound was once a volcanic lava flow.

The name possibly comes from the two Celtic words "bryn" which means a hill and "twr" which means a pile or heap of rocks hence the "tors" on Dartmoor. So "bryn twr" means a hill crag.

(3) Walk up the slope and you will soon be aware of a low bank on your left. The tracks forks here so follow round to the left into a

St Michael's Church.

gully with a low wall. These are the remains of the ramparts of an Iron Age fort or castle. Return to the track and continue the climb up and you will see below to your left the rest of the ramparts, massive and impressive earthworks built between 150 BC and AD 50 that circle round the bottom of the hill.

(4) A final steep slope to reach some granite steps, a little iron gate and into the churchyard.

The approach to Brent Tor.

The Work of the Devil at Brent Tor

St Michael's Church.

Without doubt there would have been sacred, pagan buildings on summit here from earliest times but it was not until 1130 that we read that Robert Giffard gave the Rock of Brentor so that, with the help of the monks of Tavistock, a church could be built here.

The Church of St Michael de Rupe (of the Rock) has several legends associated with its construction. One claims that originally the church was meant to be built at the foot of the tor. Work started there but every night the Devil carried all the stones to the top. The next day the builders carried all the stones down and stated the foundations once more but sure enough when night came the Devil took them all the way back to the top. Eventually the builders got so fed up with carting the stones down each day, they let the Devil have his own way and built the church on the top. Others say that the local people got so exasperated that they asked for help from the Archangel St Michael who threw a rock at the Devil that hit him on the head so that he went off in a huff!

Another legend has it that a wealthy merchant was caught in a terrible and ferocious storm while sailing back into Plymouth Sound. It looked as if his ship was about to sink so he went down on his knees on the heaving deck and prayed saying that he would

Traditonally churches built on prominent landmarks are dedicated to St Michael. Mysterious ley lines are said to run from Cornwall to Norfolk linking such sites together.

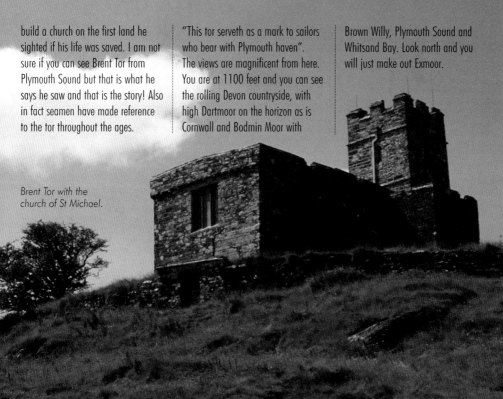

build a church on the first land he sighted if his life was saved. I am not sure if you can see Brent Tor from Plymouth Sound but that is what he says he saw and that is the story! Also in fact seamen have made reference to the tor throughout the ages.

"This tor serveth as a mark to sailors who bear with Plymouth haven". The views are magnificent from here. You are at 1100 feet and you can see the rolling Devon countryside, with high Dartmoor on the horizon as is Cornwall and Bodmin Moor with

Brown Willy, Plymouth Sound and Whitsand Bay. Look north and you will just make out Exmoor.

Brent Tor with the church of St Michael.

The stained glass window of St Michael.

A remarkable church with all around it history, legends and fantastic views, on a good day of course!

Memorial tablet for Walter Batten buried on April 6th 1677.

There is a lot to see both inside and outside this little church said to be the fourth smallest parish church in England. There is an old sundial, an extraordinary memorial tablet and another for the wife of Laurens Van de Post who came from the Giffard family. There are stories told of the difficulties of reaching the church on stormy days with the pastor having to crawl on all fours to get to the door, mourners and the parson almost being knocked over by the ferocious, howling north-east wind and having to hop like frogs to the graveside at a funeral which was conducted in the lee of the gravestones.

Memorial for the wife of Laurens van de Post Ingret Stella nee Giffard.

6 Great Grimpen Mire

*The Hound of the Baskervilles, an ancient cross,
the death of a hunter and an old farm.*

Make sure you find the right starting place in an old quarry to leave your car and are not confused by the first track coming in from your right.

This spectacular walk is amongst the most demanding in this book and is best undertaken in dry weather. But for the more adventurous walker and one to wishes to savour the unique atmosphere of this part of Dartmoor, there is no better time to walk this route than when the mist lies close upon the surrounding hills

Level: 🌸 🌸
Length: 2 miles.
Terrain: Tracks and paths.
Park & Start: Ref. SX604708
Refreshments: In Princetown.

Great
Grimpen
Mire

Childe's
Tomb +

Drainage Bottom

7

🚗 1

2

Siward's
Cross
†

6

5   4   3

Settlement   Nun's Cross
Farm

Fox Tor Mire from near the start.

1. Set off south along the track from the quarry.

After a while you will see a great marshy basin off to you left. This is the great quaking boggy marsh of Fox Tor Mire and it is said that Conan Doyle had this in mind when he wrote about Great Grimpen Mire in *The Hound of the Baskervilles*. He used to stay at Tor Royal the large mansion you passed on the way to the start.

The track at the start of the walk.

Fox Tor Mire (Great Grimpen Mire).

If you look away to the far side of Fox Tor Mire you might just make out in the distance a stone cross standing on a granite plinth. This is Childe's Tomb. Childe was a hunter who died in a terrible storm and blizzard crossing Dartmoor and, trying to shelter, he killed his horse and crept into the still warm carcase but it was no good.

Before he died he wrote in blood on a sheet of parchment that whoever gave his body a Christian burial could have all his lands. Some monks from Buckland Abbey crossing the moor days later found the body and buried it and there are records of the lands of a man called Childe being passed on to Buckland Abbey.

The track leading to Nun's Cross Farm.

There are people who have been walking along this track where you are now in thick, dead white mist who have suddenly been aware of a distant sound of a plainsong chant and seen black ghostly figures of monks carrying a bier with a body on it that fade away into distance. Childe on his way to a Christian burial?

2 You soon reach a grassy area of rough fields with an old farmhouse on the other side. This is

Sir Arthur Conan Doyle created his novel The Hound of the Baskervilles *from a number of local legends. It was originally serialised in* Strand *magazine in 1901-2.*

Nun's Cross Farm.

Nun's Cross Farm The land around here was a typical "newtake", that is land taken and improved from moorland, in this case by a John Hooper in 1870. The story goes that if you could build a dwelling and have a fire burning in the hearth in 24 hours you could claim the land around. The farm you see now quite clearly was not the little thatched croft that John Hooper must have put up then but a more recent addition.

Siward's Cross.

 If you went across the fields to look at the farm you must now walk back to the large cross that you will have seen to your right. This is Nun's Cross or Siward's Cross. It is one of the earliest crosses on Dartmoor and mentioned in 1240 as a boundary marker of Dartmoor Forest. Siward was Earl of Northumberland and owned two local manors. The cross was to mark his land. Look closely and you can just make out his name carved on one side and Boc Lond on the other that refers to Buckland Abbey whose lands came this far.

You can see that the cross has been broken. In 1846 two local lads out looking for cattle knocked it down and broke it. They were made to pay for a

local stone mason, John Newcombe, to repair it with metal clamps.

Go on west now and down through a series of gullies

The ruins of the miner's cottage.

The Devonport Leat emerging from the tunnel

until you reach a little ruin nestling against the bank. This was probably a tinners' shelter and the fine fireplace is still visible.

Just off to your left you will find the tunnel built in the 1790s from which emerges the Devonport Leat that has run underground from just south of

Nun's Cross Farm. What an incredible feat of engineering to blast through the hillside with the correct levels to maintain the flow of the leat. Indeed the

The route west.

whole leat was an extraordinary enterprise taking its water from three rivers north of the prison at Princetown and flowing as it did in the 1790s to Devonport to supply water mainly to the ships in Royal Naval Dockyard there. Some of the French prisoners of war from the Napoleonic Wars worked on it and there was a little porcelain face of a doll let into the walls of the leat until it was vandalised, put there by the

French. They probably preferred working on the leat rather than being shut up in the dank damp cells of the prison with open windows at Princetown.

5 Walk along near the leat that flows in quite a deep gully. There are quite a few paths to follow at different levels. On a bend standing high above the leat you will come to a modern granite cross fixed into a socket in a boulder. It is a memorial to a Dartmoor lover S L Hutchinson and is inscribed SLH 1887-1965.

6 Follow the leat now until you can see a track coming in from the right some way before Drivage Bottom and Older Bridge. Drivage is an old word that the miners used for tunnelling.

A sluice gate on the Devonport leat.

The modern cross with Sharpitor beyond.

7 Turn and walk up the track which is quite rough going until you reach the road. Turn right and follow the road back to the quarry and your car.

7 The Ghost of Jan Coo

*A carriage drive, Jan Coo, a smugglers'
lookout and a stone to rest coffins on.*

If you stop at the Tavistock Inn you will be drinking in a bar that the Devil visited on Sunday October 21st 1638. A tall, dark, sinister stranger called and asked for a pint and paid for it in gold. As he drank the beer it went down with a sizzling noise, as if quenching flames, that made the locals draw back in horror and astonishment. The Devil, for it was indeed him, swept out of the bar and they heard his horse galloping away to Widecombe. Later when the landlady opened the till, after drawing many pints to calm the shattered nerves of her customers, she discovered that the gold had turned to withered, autumnal leaves. The Devil went on, of course, to carry off

Level: 🥾 🥾
Length: 3 miles
Terrain: Tracks, paths, moorland.
Park & start: Ref. SX707716.
Refreshments: Tavistock Inn
Poundsgate, Badgers Holt, Dartmeet.

Jan Reynolds from Widecombe church as you will have read in Walk 2.

This is a linear walk so you will need someone to come round to Dartmeet to pick you up at the end or arrange to have two cars with one at each end. Or you could always walk back. The views always look different.

Map:

Dartmeet

Dartmoor Way

6

Sharp Tor ▲ 5

4 ▲ Bel Tor

Settlement ⚬

Rowbrook House ■

Mel Tor ▲ 3

Luckey Tor ▲

Doctor Blackall's Drive

2

Poundsgate

■ Tavistock Inn

1 🚌

Venford Brook

Bench Tor ▲

River Dart

Venford Reservoir

The Tavistock Inn.

 1 Walk up steeply through the bracken to the broad track called Dr Blackall's Drive. This was built over 150 years ago by the enterprising doctor who lived at Spitchwick Manor so that he could drive along it in his carriage and enjoy the marvellous view in all weathers.

2 Follow the track as it climbs gently north west overlooking the glorious wooded gorge of the Double Dart. There was a thriving charcoal industry in the woods here. On the far side you can see the low squat shape of Bench Tor and Venford Reservoir. Low down by the river you might just make out the rocks of Luckey Tor or Eagle Rock as it is called by some. Luckey is probably a corruption of Lookout as it is said that it is

Dr Blackall's Drive.

Looking down on the Dart with Bench Tor above.

where smugglers running contraband up the secret paths by the Dart kept an eye out for the Customs men.

(3) You will soon reach Mel Tor to your left and it is worth diverting to look out from here at another fine view. Across the shallow valley on this side you can see Rowbrook House and Rowbrook farm.

Rowbrook House.

It was at that farm that a young man called Jan Coo worked as an apprentice. One night he came in for supper in a terrible state saying that he had heard a voice crying his name Jan Coo

Rowbrook Farm where Jan Coo lived.

over and over again. Everyone rushed down to the river thinking that someone might be in trouble but they found nobody. However night after night all through the

The Double Dart gorge with Rowbrook House and Sharp Tor in the distance.

Venton Reservoir glimpsed from Mel Tor.

winter the voice went on crying "Jan Coo. Jan Coo" until poor Jan was quite demented. For a while in spring it stopped but then in summer when Jan and another farm worker were plodding up the hill for supper the voice came again. Jan turned and ran as if possessed until he reached the river and started to wade desperately across until he disappeared in the dusk and the valley was silent except the deep rumble of the river. They never found his body.

Sharp Tor is one of four tors so named on the moor. This one overlooking the Dart Valley is most aptly named from its shape. It is surrounded by prehistoric field systems and other ancient remains.

The Coffin Stone.

Carving on the Coffin Stone.

Perhaps the pixies had lured him away to live with them in their haunts under Langamarsh Pit. If you stand very still here at night you might hear the distant voice crying," Jan Coo, Jan Coo". Or is it a wood pigeon!?

(4) Walk on following the path between the walls that runs past Bel Tor until you reach the car park at Bel Tor Corner.

(5) Aim across the moorland below Sharp Tor until you reach the road.

(6) Now walk down the hill parallel to the road. No proper path here but there are usually enough sheep tracks to lead you down. Keep an eye out for a large flat topped boulder. This is the Coffin Stone where the bearers rested the coffins on the way to burial at Widecombe. Before 1260 they had to carry the coffins on the Lich Way to Lydford for burial (see Walk 9). If you look closely you will see initials and crosses carved on this historic stone. The split in the rock was said to be caused by lightning that struck after the coffin of a particularly unpleasant and wicked man had rested there.

(7) Down the hill now to Dartmeet with its road bridge and an old clapper bridge and a welcome cup of tea before a return the way you came or to wait for a friend to come and pick you up!

Dartmeet with the road bridge and the clapper bridge.

8 **The Evil Spirit of Squire Cabell**

Visit a ruined church with a strange tomb, a Cave Research Centre and a magnificent Abbey

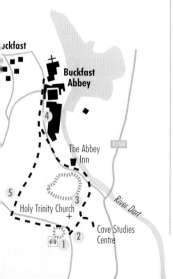

The large pipe standing in the field opposite to where you park is the shaft entrance to a cave called Baker's Pit.

The rocks underlying this area are limestone and the effect of erosion by water has created a labyrinth of caves beneath Buckfast and its neighbour Buckfastleigh. Cavers come here for underground adventures while naturalists study bats which have made the caves their home. A thousand-strong colony of the rare Greater Horseshoe bat comprises a quarter of the country's total population of these rare creatures.

Limestone is also an excellent building material and quarrying is much in evidence here. The nearby Abbey was built by a handful of monks using local stone.

Level:
Length: 1.5 miles
Terrain: Paths, fields and pavements.
Park & start: Ref. SX742665.
Refreshments: Buckfast Abbey Café. The Abbey Inn.

Buckfast Abbey

The Abbey Inn

Holy Trinity Church

River Dart

Cave Studies Centre

Walk into the churchyard through the wrought iron gate. From here it looks as if the church is still complete but it was in fact burnt down by arsonists in 1992 that, it was alleged, were Satanists performing black magic rituals. Just the shell remains. However the walls and columns and the spire were in such good condition that with maintenance and care the ruins remain while weather and time have turned it into a peaceful and beautiful place.

To the left of the porch there is a squat, white building with a wrought-iron grill on the far side through which you can see a flat-topped rectangular tomb. This is the tomb of Squire Cabell a huntsman and an appallingly evil man who had sold his soul to the Devil. He died in 1677 and was buried in the churchyard here but he was such a tormented man that his spirit could not rest so it was said that great black, howling hounds would gather round the grave and with a red, flickering glow his ghost would emerge. With

Remains of Buckfastleigh Church.

Tomb of Squire Cabell.

Inside the ruins of Buckfastleigh Church.

The ruins of an earlier church.

The steps leading down to the lane.

shrieks and unearthly howls the phantom pack with Squire Cabell would move off to hunt the country-side along the Abbot's Way. To see the spectre would mean that you would die within the year. The solid building with its grill around the tomb was supposed to prevent the phantom from escaping.

2. Go down the path eastwards in the graveyard by the ruins of an older church until you reach a gate and beyond steep steps that will lead you down to the deep set lane which in spring is full of wild garlic. Turn left.

After a short distance, ignore for now a left branch of the path but go on down to a bend where you will see a gate and a sign for a public footpath on your right. Go through the gate and you will find the William Pengelly Cave Studies Trust Centre. There is a Museum here and you can look down on the quarry that exposed a whole line of caves some of which contain bat breeding colonies and another, the Joint Mitnor Cave, has an amazing talus cone with many fossilised bones of creatures that roamed this area of Devon 112,000 years ago. In Reeds Cavern explored by and named after a well known local grocer Edgar Reed who was a caver, there is a queer little stalagmite that looks like a man with a top hat which is said to be directly under the tomb of Squire Cabell and represents his soul. You can get details of Guided Walks and entry to the caves and Museum by contacting 01752 700293 or 01752 775195.

The Pengelly Cave Centre.

Memorial to Edgar Reed.

Cave entrance in the quarry at the Caving Centre.

Squire Cabell was the inspiration for Conan Doyle's family named Baskerville who are terrorised by a gigantic hound on Dartmoor. The real-life Baskerville was coachman who drove the author around the moor.

3 Back now the way you came through the gate and walk up to the bend you passed earlier and turn right. Go through the open iron gate and follow the deep set path steeply down with quite a number of steps.

4 You will now emerge at the road by a huge quarry on the left and opposite the Abbey Inn.

The Abbey Inn.

Follow the pavement beside the road to Buckfast Abbey.

Obviously it is impossible to give a history of the Abbey here but there are records that suggest that it was founded in 1018 by Benedictines, but by 1147 the monks here were now Cistercians who were wool traders who used the Abbot's Way to take wool over to Buckland and Tavistock Abbeys. In 1539 came the Dissolution of the Abbeys and Buckfast fell into disrepair and ruin until nothing

remained. In 1882 Bendictines came back and built a temporary church and in 1897 the monks began to make their famous tonic wine! By 1907 they started to rebuild the Abbey with only six monks working on it at any one time and by 1938 the building was completed. There is a lot to see here and a visit is essential.

5 Walk back the way you came until you see a sign low down to your right marked Public Footpath by St Mary's Catholic Primary School . Follow that road up to the bend where straight ahead of you there is a leafy lane which once again becomes deep cut path. Finally go through an iron gate into some fields and you will reach a road where you turn left to get back to your car by the church.

Steps on the path leading down to the road.

Buckfast Abbey.

9 **The Hairy Hands**

The Hairy Hands, the path of the dead and a Gunpowder Factory.

Level: 🥾 🥾
Length: 2.5 miles.
Terrain: Paths and open moor.
Park & start: Ref. SX635771.
Refreshments: Powder Mills & Princetown.

Just back from the car park the road bridge goes over the Cherry Brook which rises high on the north moor and later joins the Dart. An odd name this that comes from the Old English Churybrok with its derivation from "Cyric" meaning a barrow or burial place.

The bend in the road over the bridge has a sinister reputation. There have been many road accidents here with both cars and motor bikes over the years and those that have lived have all told macabre stories of strange, malignant forces at work often in the form of hairy hands pulling at the steering wheel or closing over their own hands to wrench the wheel to one side making them swerve and drive off the road. Nobody knows why there should be these manifestations and psychic powers here.

In Bellever Forest.

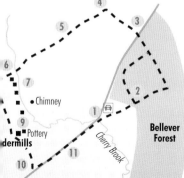

• Chimney

• Pottery

dermills

Bellever Forest

Cherry Brook

55

1 If you managed to park safely without driving off the road go through the gate on the far side and set off up the quite badly eroded path. Soon you will reach a gate and a stile to enter the forest.

2 At the broad ride you can turn left and follow that or keep straight on into the forest. This track becomes very muddy and rutted even in dry weather. When you reach the cross roads turn left and walk on

down a delightful track until you reach the broad ride that you might have followed. If you came on the broad track turn left or if you came the other way keep straight on down to the road.

The Cherry Brook Corner.
Hairy Hand Corner.

The Lich Way through the forest.

(3) Go through the gate and cross the road and go through the other gate onto the open moor.

You are now on the Lich Way. This extraordinary track runs right across Dartmoor and was used by mourners from the Ancient Tenements carrying the coffins of the dead for burial at Lydford which as you read in Walk 4 was the main parish church on Dartmoor; what an appalling journey it must have been in wind, rain and snow. People talk about a strange atmosphere of deep grief and sorrow when walking the Lich Way and of seeing shrouded figures in the mist. However in 1260 Bishop Bronescombe gave permission for the

The Lich Way crossing the causeway.

A 19th century worker at Powdermills, one Silas Sleep, was said to eat his packed breakfast and dinner at the same time so that if he were blown up during the day he would at least meet his maker 'fully replenished'.

The gate leading to Powder Mills.

inhabitants in the south eastern part of Dartmoor to take their coffins to Widecombe on the Church Way (see Walk 7).

4 Follow the old causeway across the bog. It can become very muddy in wet weather.

5 On the far side swing left on a fairly indistinct track and aim towards the old television mast

on North Hessary Tor. There are small white and blue waymarks to follow.

6 Aim for the brow of the hill and look for the gate through the wall. You will now be in an extraordinary area of odd looking

View across Powder Mills.

Water-wheel house where the powder was ground in the mill.

ruins and chimneys. This is Powder Mills where gunpowder was made by an enterprise started by Mr George Frean in 1844. You can see the ruins of three massive water-wheel houses that used water brought by interconnecting leats. Gunpowder was in great demand in the quarries, tin mines and by farmers and was produced here by grinding very finely sulphur, saltpetre and charcoal.

The buildings were all a long way from other dwellings as the risk of accidental explosions was high and indeed there were quite a few disasters. Some of the buildings had roofs made of tarred canvas so that in the event of their being blown off they could be replaced more easily than

Water-wheel pit.

conventional roofs. With the invention of dynamite the production of gunpowder declined and by the 1890s Powder Mills had closed. Follow the track down the hill.

(7) Cross the bridge over the upper reaches of the Cherry Brook and turn right and climb up past a chimney built to discharge fumes from drying the gunpowder and go through the gate onto the open moor. Looking at the expanse of open

Another of three wheel house mills.

The distinctive ruined chimney at Powder Mills built to discharge fumes from drying the gunpowder.

The gate out beside the pottery.

moor ahead of you imagine still having to carry a coffin another nine miles to Lydford.

8 Turn left and follow the wall and fence down behind the buildings one of which was the manager's house for the mills.

The mortar for testing the gunpowder.

9 Go through the gate on your left and you will see the Pottery which is worth visiting and where you can get cream teas in the summer.

10 Walk south now along the drive. You will pass the mortar on your right that was fired to test the efficiency of the gunpowder produced.

11 Turn left and walk along the grass verge back to your car.

10 **The Phantom Roman Soldiers**

A stone nut cracker, a hill-top fort, phantom Romans and a deep wooded cleave

ntil recent times it was commonly believed that the Roman occupation of the Westcountry stopped at Exeter and that they ventured further west only in small numbers. This was based on the apparent lack of archaeological evidence of Roman presence west of the River Exe. We now know this is not the case as more and more artefacts come to light. Indeed, quite recently a Roman coin was found on the hillfort at Hunter's Tor - part of this walk. Thus the legend of a cohort of Roman soldiers marching into the valley below the hillfort is not so far-fetched as it might once have been!

Challenging in some of the steeper climbs, this is one of the most beautiful walks on the edge of the moor, with superb views.

Level: 🥾 🥾
Length: 3.5 miles.
Terrain: Tracks, paths, open moor.
Park & start: Ref. SX775816.
Refreshments: Lustleigh.

Map labels

6

5 Iron Age Fort

Hunter's 4 Tor

Raven's Tor 3

8

Lustleigh Cleave 9

River Bovey

2 1

Iron Age Ramparts.

(1) Park near Hammerslake marked on the OS map and follow the signs for Hunter's Tor. The deep cut path opens out and then climbs quite steeply up a wooded slope littered with great granite rocks.

(2) Soon you will see to your left boulders that are called Sharpitor. There was once a logan stone here and, as is often the case, it

The deep cut path at the start.

was called the nut crackers. There are stories told of local people coming up here at Christmas to crack their nuts under the logan stone for good luck.

The track levels out.

(3) The track levels out bearing right onto a plateau with a feeling of space with huge skies. Below you to your left is the lovely wooded Lustleigh Cleave and amazing views across to Dartmoor.

(4) The path leads you through a lot of granite boulders to the remains of the ramparts and ditches of an Iron Age Fort but local legend

tells of a mysterious troop of Roman legionaires haunting the summit. They are seen only on bright moonlit nights marching in close formation in full military dress with their standards carried with them. The manifestations seem to glow in the moonlight and cries of battle, in Latin of course, float eerily across the rocks and ramparts. Whether the Iron Age inhabitants of the fort fought a battle here with the Romans is not known but certainly the Romans advanced as far west as North Tawton on the road that they built into the area.

Granite outcrops on the plateau with Low Man and Haytor in the background.

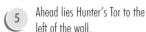

5 Ahead lies Hunter's Tor to the left of the wall.

6 Set off through the gate in the wall and drop steeply down the path through the bracken in summer to Peck Farm.

7 Go through the gate follow the path past the farm and walk down the drive to the lane where you turn left to Foxworthy Bridge down more deep cut ancient paths.

8 At Foxworthy Farm follow the signs to Hammerslake that will take you into the glorious, deep wooded valley of Lustleigh Cleave with the sound of the River Bovey to your right. Keep on below Raven's Tor and then past Foxes Yard; always keep straight on at any path junctions.

Foxworthy.

Talking of foxes there is a final legend about a group of huntsmen in Tudor costumes with their pack of hounds that can be seen in broad daylight in summer riding up the Cleave or sometimes emerging on the heights of Hunter's Tor; is this the reason for the name I wonder? The phantoms vanish in an instant and the baying of the hounds and the distant horn fades into the distance.

9 Climb gently up through the trees and follow the wall then turn right down the gully back to your car.

Hunter's Tor.